ANIMAL FAMILIES

by

Sally King

Illustrated by Jacqueline Tee

Grosvenor House
Publishing Limited

The right of Sally King to be identified as the author of this
work has been asserted in accordance with Section 78
of the Copyright, Designs and Patents Act 1988

The book cover picture is copyright to Sally King

This book is published by
Grosvenor House Publishing Ltd
Link House
140 The Broadway, Tolworth, Surrey, KT6 7HT.
www.grosvenorhousepublishing.co.uk

A CIP record for this book
is available from the British Library

ISBN 978-1-78623-886-3

Reading in Rhyme
Animal Families

To remember our names you must endeavour,
And then you will be so very clever.

CONTENTS

PIG

A mother pig is called a SOW.

I don't know how, but she is a SOW.

Baby PIGLET sleeps and plays.

This is how he spends his days.

He makes a noise, a sniffle or snore,

Like his Dad, the bigger BOAR.

A sniffle or snort, a grunt or a squeal,

He snuffles about to find every meal.

We live in a STY. That's our home by and by,

With a gate and walls that are not very high.

We lie in mud, with straw and hay,

Sunbathing, sleeping, every day.

I am Mum, the SOW.

You know that now.

My tiny pet

Is baby PIGLET.

What's even more,

Dad is the BOAR.

We don't know why

But we live in a STY.

To remember our names you must endeavour,

And then you will be so very clever.

SHEEP

A mother sheep is called a EWE.

I don't mean you. She is called a EWE.

Her baby LAMB sleeps and plays.

This is how he spends his days.

With wool on his back, grass he eats,

Jumps and frolics, baas and bleats.

But his Dad, the RAM, he needs some space,

For he has curled horns around his face.

We can live in a PEN, that's our home, our den,

With a field of grass, where we go now and then.

We can sleep in the field, in the shade of a tree,

And we grow wool on our backs to make jumpers, you see.

I am Mum, the EWE, not you, but a EWE.

You may not believe it but it's true.

The male is a RAM, the dad we said,

The one with the horns upon his head.

The baby's a LAMB, a sweet little thing,

With his jumping and frolicking and plaintive bleating.

And you remember the PEN and the FIELD of grass,

And the baas and the bleats as the shepherds pass?

To remember our names you must endeavour,

And then you will be so very clever.

GOAT

A mother goat, NANNY is what I am called,

Not a granny or grandma, or someone old,

Or a job in childcare I do not hold.

My baby, a KID, sleeps and plays.

This is how he spends his days.

He sounds like a lamb. He bleats and cries,

And this is going to be a surprise.

It does sound rather awfully silly,

But my KID's Dad is called a BILLY.

He is big and strong and eats everything.

Your hat, your coat, a piece of string.

His kick is hard. With his horns he will butt.

We live in a PEN, a field or a hut.

A sturdy family who can live outside,

We just need some shelter from cold to hide.

The Mum is NANNY, the Dad is BILLY,

The baby is a KID. That does sound silly

Because so are you, a KID, a child.

But you, like us, are not so wild.

To remember our names you must endeavour,

And then you will be so very clever.

COW

A mother cow is called a COW.

That seems rather silly now.

Her baby CALF sleeps and plays.

This is how he spends his days.

The noise he makes is called a MOO.

A long Mmmmmmm. That will do.

We chew on grass until we're full.

The father cow, he is the BULL.

A heavy chap, with ring through nose,

What's that for, do you suppose?

We sleep in a BYRE, a barn or a shed,

And the Dad, the BULL, by his nose is led.

That ring in his nose, with a rope pulled through,

That is what the farmers do.

We eat the grass and give you milk,

Creamy and as smooth as silk,

Me, I am the COW,

And you know that now.

And my baby CALF.

He makes you laugh.

Dad, the BULL, bigger and higher,

We all live together in a BYRE.

To remember our names you must endeavour,

And then you will be so very clever.

WHALE

Well, here is another.

COW is the mother.

We already know,

From some time ago,

That a male cow is a BULL

And he stands large and full.

A male whale, a BULL, the same.

It has the same name

And the same sort of build

As that bull in the field.

And, as before, when learning how

The family of cow

Was cow, bull and calf,

Well, this makes us laugh,

That the whale is the same,

So who can we blame

For making the mother whale COW,

The father a BULL, and how

Crazy by half,

Baby whale is a CALF!

My CALF likes to swim in the ocean and play.

This is how he spends his day.

We keep warm in the sea because we have blubber

Like a layer of dense India rubber.

Thick fat lies under our skin,

That is why we can never be thin.

We have COW, BULL and CALF you see,

For mum, dad and whale baby.

To remember our names you must endeavour,

And then you will be so very clever.

CRAB

Do you remember a JENNY is a female ass?

If so, go straight to the top of the class.

Now I'm going to tell you something new,

A female crab is a JENNY too!

Yes, JENNY is my name. A mother crab.

With my pincers I grab and I stab and I jab.

I have a hard shell and sideways I stagger,

My claws are sharp too. As sharp as a dagger.

I have no backbone. I am a crustacean,

With ten legs I can move quickly through the ocean.

My baby, a ZOEA, is smaller than me.

He likes to swim, splashing in the sea.

Splashing and running, he likes to play,

And this is how he spends his day.

Dad is a JIMMY, a very fine chap

Who folds into his shell when needing a nap.

You can find us on land, in the sand or a pool,

Buried deep we hide, keeping safe, keeping cool.

JENNY and JIMMY crab and baby ZOEA,

My goodness! You are learning some new names here!

To remember our names you must endeavour,

And then you will be so very clever.

CAT

A mother cat am I. A QUEEN, don't you know.

I hold my head up high, royal, a QUEEN from head to toe.

My baby KITTENS mew and play.

This is how they spend their day.

They open their eyes at ten days old

And their sight is not good, for so I am told.

Their father is the TOM, the male,

He hunts at night, with swishing tail,

Stalking his prey, he prowls in the dark,

Roaming his territory, making his mark.

Quite often he gets into a fight

With another TOM cat. They hiss and they bite.

They fight it out and then without doubt,

They'll meet again for another bout.

He limps home again with missing fur,

But, seeing us, he starts to purr,

With bloodied ear that's ripped and torn,

He brings himself in, somewhat forlorn,

Lies by the fire, licks himself clean,

With never a thought to where he has been.

We can live in a home with a family kind

Or on a farm, in a barn, we do not mind.

The QUEEN, the TOM and the KITTENS too,

So there you are. And whatever you do,

Don't forget our names, will you?

To remember our names you must endeavour,

And then you will be so very clever.

HORSE

A mother horse is called a MARE.

I don't know where that came from. MARE.

Baby FOAL sleeps and plays.

This is how he spends his days.

He neighs. He plays.

He runs, jumps and stays

Beside his mother's side, the MARE.

And this is where

We must meet the STALLION, father horse

I think you've heard of him, of course.

Black as night, he is tall and proud,

And when he neighs, it's very loud.

He whinnies, he puffs and snorts and neighs,

He shows his power in many ways.

We live in a STABLE, with fresh straw and hay.

What shall we have for dinner today?

Oats and bran; we like grass too,

Carrots and apples, just like you.

Well, I am the MARE.

My mane is my hair.

The baby horse, my baby FOAL,

The STALLION, his father, as black as coal.

We live in a field of grass or a stable.

A horse's home bears that label.

To remember our names you must endeavour,

And then you will be so very clever

SEAHORSE

A seahorse is, of course,
A sort of horse.
So, can you imagine
The male is a stallion?
We call him SEA STALLION, his wife is SEA MARE,
And don't they make the perfect pair?
Just like the horse you see in a stable,
Or read about in a story or fable.
The baby, no foal, no colt or filly,
For it would sound so very silly
To have a SEA MARE, SEA STALLION, sea foal,
The tiny sea horse is a sweet little soul.
We call him a FRY. No, not something you take,
And fry in a pan like a huge pancake.
We call him a FRY because he's so small,
Sometimes only half an inch tall.
Seahorses are fish but they look equine,
They live in salt water, the sea, the brine.
The strange thing to know, this is a true fact,
The male has the babies. This is the pact
Made between sea stallion and sea mare.
I told you they were an amazing pair.

The fry appear fully grown from eggs,
And at birth, off they swim on their own sea legs.
So just think what you've learned about seahorses so small,
A little fish, not a horse at all.
To remember our names you must endeavour,
And then you will be so very clever.

FALCON

A bird of prey indeed I am,

Soaring through the skies,

Spotting my kill from far away,

I dive to win my prize.

They call me FALCON, the female bird,

The male has a different name,

He is a TIERCEL, smaller than I,

He dives with only one aim.

That is to hunt throughout the day

To feed our EYAS, our chick.

There is no other bird in the world today

Who, in a dive, can be as quick.

The EYAS waits for food. High up in the nest he stays.

And this is how he grows and how he spends his days.

Watching the fastest birds on earth,

He learns as much as he can,

Our nests are up high on cliff top ledges

To escape our one enemy, man.

So remember our names if you are able,

FALCON, TIERCEL and EYAS all three,

Supreme hunters of the avian world,

Birds of prey, fast and free.

To remember our names you must endeavour,

And then you will be so very clever.

GOOSE

A mother goose... well, she is a GOOSE.

That name I did not choose.

Just GOOSE.

GOSLING is my baby bird.

Is that a name that you have heard?

My baby GOSLING sleeps and plays.

This is how he spends his days.

He makes a noise, a spit, a hiss,

If you can do so, give him a miss.

Sometimes he honks, a funny call,

Sitting on the farmyard wall.

His Dad, the GANDER, is not your friend,

If you go near him, he will send

You running, wings outspread.

Geese will attack you, did you hear what I said?

They guard the farmyard, lay some eggs,

Watch out for burglars, snap at their legs.

So do take care. GOOSE, GOSLING, GANDER,

Into their territory do not wander.

To remember our names you must endeavour,

And then you will be so very clever.

TURKEY

A mother goose is called a goose,
A mother duck is duck,
A mother hen is called a hen,
But a turkey, no such luck.
A baby goose is called a gosling,
A baby duckling we all have met,
A baby hen is called a chick,
But a baby turkey you don't know yet.
A father goose is called a gander,
A father duck, a drake,
The cockerel is the father hen,
But a turkey... for goodness sake!
Now you feel a bit confused
So we shall learn the name.
The mother turkey is a HEN
Just like the hen, the same.
The baby POULT he likes to play
And this is how he spends his day,
He follows the others on the farm
And the GOBBLER, his dad, keeps him from harm.
Male turkeys make a 'gobble' noise,
As they sit in the yard and wait
For the farmer to throw the daily corn,

That's where dad's name might originate.
When a group of turkeys are huddled together
A RAFTER of turkeys they are called,
And as they grow and fatten up,
Some say they look ugly, some say bald.
The fleshy red bit hanging off the beak
This is called a 'snood'.
I don't much like the look of it
But I wouldn't want to sound rude.
So now you know them
GOBBLER, HEN and POULT all three,
Perhaps those names you can
Commit to your memory.
To remember our names you must endeavour,
And then you will be so very clever.

CHIMPANZEE

EMPRESS is a female chimpanzee.

Noble by birth. Can't you see?

INFANT babies, like you when small,

But not at Infant School, no, not at all.

My baby INFANT swings and plays.

This is how he spends his days.

He climbs the trees and laughs with chatter,

Sometimes he falls, but it doesn't matter.

I catch him. Or sometimes his dad, keeping guard at night,

The BLACKBACK, will reach out and hold him tight.

We live in the jungle in quite large groups,

In families of thirty or eighty, we call them TROOPS.

Troops of monkeys, apes or chimpanzees,

So remember us now, if you please.

EMPRESS, the female, BLACKBACK the male,

And with his chatter and a wail

There's INFANT baby too.

Sometimes found inside a zoo.

To remember our names you must endeavour,

And then you will be so very clever.

SWAN

A stately mother swan am I,

Look out for me as I swim by.

A PEN. My name is a PEN.

Do you remember when,

With my long, white neck, I came,

And you did not know my name?

Gliding past you, throwing bread, or

The white feathered bird, honking overhead.

My babies, CYGNETS, ugly and grey,

They will be beautiful one day.

Ugly ducklings it has been said,

When people come to throw us bread.

The baby CYGNETS swim and play.

This is how they spend their day.

Amongst the rushes of the river

Where we build our nests in all kinds of weather.

And in the Winter we fly away,

For in the cold we cannot stay.

You may see us flying overhead, a mob

Of feathered creatures. The male, the COB,

Leads the flock to a warmer place.

I will return in Spring and show my face.

Mother swan is PEN, the COB is the male,

Baby CYGNETS will turn white as they sail

Through water of rivers, lakes and seas.

Do not forget us, if you please.

To remember our names you must endeavour,

And then you will be so very clever.

HARE

I'm a mother hare. A DOE or a JILL,

Like the two in the rhyme who went up the hill.

Dad is the JACK or the BUCK. He's bigger than I

And he leaps and he bounds right up to the sky.

A baby hare has a peculiar name.

A LEVERET, and we're not terribly tame.

We live in the wild, on moors and hills,

A collection, a DROVE, of JACKs and JILLs.

Little LEVERET loves to jump and play.

This is how he spends his day.

We build a nest, a dip in the ground,

Where we sit and rest. Safe and sound.

A nest on the ground, to us is the norm,

Made of grass, near rocks, we call it a FORM.

Hares have long legs and very long ears.

We've developed a reputation over the years,

Some call us March hares as it is then, in the Spring,

We are said to perform in a boxing ring.

Mad March hares, in the light of the moon,

BUCK, DOE, LEVERET, you will learn our names soon.

To remember our names you must endeavour,

And then you will be so very clever.

LION, TIGER, LEOPARD

Well, here we are, three animals to name,

And all three are very much the same

The lion is LION and his partner LIONESS,

A bit like naming prince and princess.

Babies for all three it's true

Are CUBS. Like all cats they mew.

But as they grow and jump and play

And gradually spend the day,

They learn to growl and then the roars,

So frightening to see these carnivores.

With claws and teeth they hunt their food,

Meat of every kind that might be stood

Drinking at a water hole.

Look out! Don't be a fool!

What's that in the bushes?

As out the big cat rushes.

Brings its prey down to the ground

No one would choose to stick around.

TIGER's jungle habitats

Make him the largest of these cats.

His wife, the TIGRESS, hunts with him,

Unusual as it is, tigers can swim!

They have dark black stripes on orange fur,

And like all pussy cats, they probably purr

When they lie sleeping in their den,

Away from game hunters, the guns and the men.

The LEOPARD is a smaller beast,

With spots to distinguish him at least.

Leopards climb trees and like rocky places,

They prefer to hide than be in open spaces.

Leopard's speed is fast and will certainly impress

His wife, the beautiful LEOPARDESS.

Once again, CUBS are the young,

All leopards are known to be very strong

Nocturnal means they hunt at night

And tend to rest and sleep in daylight.

So here we have big cat species,

To the names of the males just add ee's and s'ss.

From LION make LIONESS,

TIGER to TIGRESS,

And, finally, LEOPARD is partnered with LEOPARDESS.

Reading about them in this little rhyme

Has meant you have learned three at the same time.

To remember our names you must endeavour,

And then you will be so very clever.

DEER

A mother deer is a DOE,

A gentle creature you know.

Her baby is a little FAWN,

And just after he is born

He stands up on his wobbly feet,

And oh! He looks so very sweet!

His father, the STAG, is tall and strong,

With huge antlers, like branches, very long

That stand upon his stately head.

Of humans they live in constant dread.

They hide in forests, a wood or a hill,

For there are hunters who will kill.

So shy and nervous. Not often seen here.

They know if those hunters with guns have been near.

My little FAWN, he sleeps and plays.

This is how he spends his days.

He stays close to his mother, the DOE,

Walking with her wherever she may go.

The mother, the DOE,

That's something you know,

The baby, the FAWN,

A word you can learn.

And the STAG, the reindeer, so stately and proud,

Just say his name, right out loud.

To remember our names you must endeavour,

And then you will be so very clever.

DONKEY

A mother donkey is a JENNY.

Have you ever heard of any

Other creature called a JENNY?

There are not many.

A baby donkey is called a FOAL,

On his back in the meadow he loves to roll,

This baby FOAL can jump and play,

This is how he spends his day.

His Dad is a JACK,

With a very strong back.

He is made to carry heavy loads

Over hills and mountain roads.

The noise we make is a great Hee Haw.

Well crows can caw and we Hee Haw.

We can be noisy if we choose.

But mostly we prefer to snooze

Or stand quietly in the sun

Not bothering anyone,

Until you come with carrots in hand,

Take us for donkey rides on the sand,

In the summer by the sea,

JACK, FOAL and mother JENNY.

To remember our names you must endeavour,

And then you will be so very clever.

FOX

A mother fox, a VIXEN, her name,

At night into your garden she came.

She has a loud and howling call.

At home, some CUBS, babies all.

The CUBS, the babies, sleep and play.

This is how they spend their day.

A litter of puppies look just the same,

Joining in each other's game

While mother's hunting in the fog

With their father. He is the DOG.

A DOG FOX and a VIXEN creep

Through the night while you sleep.

DOG and VIXEN go out for food,

Hunt rabbits and chickens, both are good.

Their home is an EARTH,

A deep hole in the ground,

Where from gamekeepers and farmers

They cannot be found,

Sometimes a hunt is out with the hounds

And they chase us back to our EARTH underground.

The mother, VIXEN. DOG FOX, sly and clever.

Can you remember them now for ever and ever?

To remember our names you must endeavour,

And then you will be so very clever.

HEDGEHOG

A pig can sometimes be called a hog.
In a similar way, a male fox is a dog.
You have learned that already in these rhymes,
So could a hedgehog be a hedgepig sometimes?
A baby hedgehog is known as a HOGLET.
A baby pig is known as a piglet.
HOGLET, piglet; the similarity is clear
And I am the SOW, the mother dear.
Just as a mother pig is also a sow,
Well, what do you think the dad could be now?
Yes, you are right. The dad is a BOAR,
So hedgehog could be hedgepig, as we mentioned before.
The HOGLET he snuffles, eats and plays,
This is how he spends his days.
We live in woodlands, gardens, a ditch, or a mire,
And can sometimes be found in a November bonfire.
In piles of leaves in the winter we sleep.
If you find us, we don't mind if you first take a peep.
But do not disturb us too much, that we hate,
Because in this cold weather we hibernate.
There we are, what a terrible muddle,
And what's more, a hedgehog you wouldn't want to cuddle.
Why? Because of his prickly spines,
And also on slugs and snails he dines.
Not the sort of family pet you need,
But their names you might like to learn indeed.
To remember our names you must endeavour,
And then you will be so very clever.

DID YOU REMEMBER OUR NAMES?

There was pig, goat and sheep,

And hedgehog fast asleep,

A fox and a cow,

Remember how

The turkey gobbles and the goose gives a hiss,

Which other animals did we miss?

A donkey, a horse,

Deer and falcon of course.

The ones in the sea,

You've reminded me.

Whale, seahorse and crab

With his jab and his stab.

The hare and the cat,

We nearly forgot that.

Then the big cats three,

And the chimpanzee.

One more to add to our list,

Which one have we missed?

It was fox, could you tell?

You did very well.

Such an endeavour!

And so very clever!

Lightning Source UK Ltd.
Milton Keynes UK
UKOW07n1403010917
308411UK00003B/7/P